Atalanta

A Full-Length Play

By

THOMAS J. HATTON

THE DRAMATIC PUBLISHING COMPANY

ATALANTA
A Full-Length Play
For Seven Men, Seven Women, Extras*

CHARACTERS

Oeneus . . . . .King of Calydon
Althea. . . . . his wife
Agatha . . . . his mother-in-law
Serendipity . . . . his daughter
Meleager . . . . .his son
Hercules
Theseus   . . . . Greek heroes
Jason
Demetrius . . . . a poet
Atalanta . . . . a Greek maiden
Cassandra
Deinera   . . . . .followers of Atalanta
Clio
Herald. . . . . secretary to Oeneus

TIME: The Present

PLACE: The little island of Calydon

*Other women followers of Atalanta.

3

ACT ONE

SCENE ONE

SCENE: The Royal Throne Room of Oeneus, King of the little island of Calydon. It is ten o'clock on a Thursday morning, the customary day and hour at which Oeneus conducts public business.

AT RISE OF CURTAIN: The stage is empty except for the HERALD, a middle-aged man, who sits at his table writing with a quill pen on a scroll. A trumpet sounds off R. OENEUS, ALTHEA and AGATHA enter R. OENEUS is a short, balding man of some forty-five years. He wears a toga trimmed in purple and a laurel wreath in his hair. He is somewhat overshadowed by ALTHEA who, although about the same age as he, is still a beauty and — unfortunately — somewhat taller than he. Both are overshadowed by AGATHA, a large Wagnerian-type woman with steel gray hair and the disposition of a tiger tank. The women wear gold-trimmed robes. The three cross to their thrones, talking, as the HERALD springs to attention.

OENEUS. I do hope court business won't take too long today. I'm just itching to get back to my latest model catapult. It's a Helenic XZ-300 used by the Thebans at Marathon.

ALTHEA. Ony, you have simply got to stop spending so

5

much time with those silly catapult models and spend
more time ruling this kingdom. Don't you realize that
we're in the midst of a crisis?

OENEUS. What crisis is that? Are the Parthians kicking up
things again?

AGATHA. No, no, Odius. It's that monstrous creature
that's ramping all about destroying the crops and ripping
up peasants with its tusks. It's the boar that the Goddess
Artremis has plagued us with. (By this time the three
have taken their seats. ALTHEA sits on Oeneus' right,
AGATHA on his left. When the royalty is seated, the
HERALD also sits and returns to his scrolls.)

OENEUS. Mother, how many times do I have to tell you?
My name is Oeneus, not Odius.

AGATHA. It'll be mud if you don't do something about that
pig. The price of bread and wine is going to go out of
sight this fall. Nobody is willing to work the land — and
I can't blame them.

ALTHEA. Oh, if only you hadn't gotten the goddess angry.

OENEUS. How did I know she would take offense? It was
an honest oversight. Somehow her name got left off the
list of dieties when I made my sacrifice, that's all. That's
the trouble with polytheism — it's such a bureaucracy.
Now, if we only had just one or two gods to worry
about . . .

ALTHEA. Well, you'd better worry about Artremis and her
pig. The people are beginning to murmur.

OENEUS. For your information, love, I have worried about
them. In fact, I've taken steps.

AGATHA. We know. You took about a thousand quick
ones to the rear when you met the boar yourself. Disgraceful conduct.

OENEUS. I was just making a strategic retreat to get my
catapult. But I really am working on the problem. In
fact, it's the first order of business today.

AGATHA. What are you going to do? Pass a law making it illegal to stab people with boar tusks and expect the pig to abide by it?

OENEUS. No, mother. Some time ago I sent messengers all over creation describing our little problem and offering a grand prize to any hero who would come here and rid us of Mr. Porkchops. And today's the day all the contenders have assembled.

ALTHEA. You offered a grand prize? What kind of grand prize do we have to offer?

AGATHA. Don't you know that our economy is on deficit spending right now? Who's joined this contest anyhow?

OENEUS. Well, let's see. Herald, give me the list of entrants.

HERALD. Yes, sire. (He crosses and hands OENEUS a scroll. OENEUS glances at it and hands it back. The HERALD returns to his seat.)

OENEUS. Some of the best. Hercules, Theseus, Jason . . .

AGATHA. Oh, that's just marvelous. One of them is just likely to kill that thing. Do you know what he'll do when he discovers he's been taken?

ALTHEA. I'm afraid he'll be twice as bad as the boar.

OENEUS. But, my love, we do have a grand prize — and a legitimate one.

ALTHEA. What in the world do we have to offer to men like those? We can't even afford heroes union scale.

OENEUS. Now that's where you're wrong. We have a wonderful grand prize right here in Calydon. To the man who kills the boar I'm giving the hand of the Princess Serendipity.

ALTHEA. Dippy? You're going to give him Dippy?

OENEUS. And half the kingdom — the poorer half, of course.

ALTHEA. But Dippy's a mere girl. Who'd be interested in her?

OENEUS. My dear, Dippy is eighteen years old — a little underdeveloped, perhaps, but still definitely eighteen. It's time she's married, and this is a perfect chance to get rid of a boar and a daughter all at once. And we'd have to give up half the kingdom as a dowery for her sooner or later anyway.

ALTHEA. You know, you might have something there.

AGATHA. I don't like it. It sounds sensible. We're always in big trouble when Odius sounds sensible.

ALTHEA. But how does Dippy feel about all this?

OENEUS. To tell you the truth, I haven't mentioned the matter to her. Thought it might be better as a surprise. But Dippy will go along with it — she's always been a dutiful daughter.

AGATHA. Sometimes I wish the girl had a little more backbone.

ALTHEA. Now, mother. You know, I think this plan just might work. It sounds to me like Ony has come up with a good idea.

AGATHA. If he has, it'll be the first time. But I suppose even he deserves a chance. Lead on, Odius. Let's see how you're going to blow this one.

OENEUS. Thank you, mother. Your confidence in me is touching. (To HERALD.) Let the applicants for the royal boar hunt be announced.

(The HERALD steps R and reads off the names of the applicants. As each applicant's name is read, he enters R, crosses to the thrones, kneels before OENEUS, then rises and steps back to form a line facing the audience UC. HERCULES, THESEUS and JASON are large, athletic men. HERCULES wears a lion's skin and carries a club. THESEUS and JASON wear Greecian armor and carry spears. DEMETRIUS is a slight, artistic-looking young man. He wears a toga and carries a light bow.)

HERALD. The noble Hercules, son of Zeus, slayer of lions,

conqueror of the hydra, cleaner of the Aegean Stables, et cetera, et cetera, et cetera. The noble Theseus, Prince of Athens, slayer of the Minotaur, conqueror of the Amazons, et cetera, et cetera, et cetera. The noble Jason, son of Aeson, commander of the Argonauts, winner of the Golden Fleece, et cetera, et cetera. Demetrius, son of Homer, court poet.

OENEUS (as DEMETRIUS advances). Poet? Poet? What's a poet doing here?

DEMETRIUS. Your Majesty, I have decided to forsake the muses for Mars. I have put aside my pen and taken up the sword.

OENEUS. But you don't even have an *et cetera* to your name.

DEMETRIUS. A man has to start some place, your Majesty. Your heralds said the contest was open to anyone.

OENEUS. Well, it's your funeral. If you think you can beat out these all-stars here . . . next, Herald.

HERALD. Meleager, son of Oeneus.

ALTHEA. Mel?

(MELEAGER enters and kneels. He is a young man of roughly twenty-two, dressed like THESEUS and JASON.)

OENEUS. Now come on, Meleager. You can't take part in this contest. You're my son.

MELEAGER. The rules say nothing about relatives of the sponsor being excluded, father. As your son, I feel it is my duty to uphold the honor of Calydon. We should be able to solve our problems without calling in outsiders. Besides, I want to inherit all of your kingdom, not just half of it.

OENEUS. But you're supposed to be in Athens, at school.

MELEAGER. It's semester break.

AGATHA. Odius, you can't let him go out after that monster. It's too dangerous.

OENEUS. Now, look here, Meleager. You know the prize in
    this contest is the hand of the Princess Serendipity. Now
    I don't know what they've been teaching you up there in
    Athens, but here in Calydon we frown on brothers and
    sisters getting married.

MELEAGER. Oh, for heavens sake, father. I wouldn't want
    to marry Dippy. I just want to keep the honor of Calydon
    intact — not to mention the kingdom.

ALTHEA. Ony, you're not going to let him risk his life.
    He's not a fighter — he's a student.

MELEAGER. Mother, I'm a four-letter man at college. I'm
    on the first string at discus throwing.

OENEUS. Really, Althea, I don't see how I can stop the
    boy. There's nothing in the rules. Besides, he has a nice
    point about keeping the kingdom intact.

AGATHA. Well, I don't like it. This idea of yours is starting
    to turn out like all the others.

OENEUS. Let's get on with the introduction of the heroes.
    Herald . . .

HERALD. There's only one more, your Majesty. (He raises
    his voice.) Atalanta, the fair, slayer of satyrs.

(MELEAGER joins the other contestants. ATALANTA
    enters and kneels. She is a pretty, athletic-looking girl
    of about twenty. She wears a white tunic, a short white
    skirt and sandals. She wears a bow and quiver of arrows
    over her shoulders.)

OENEUS. But . . . but you're a girl.

ATALANTA (rising). Yes, your Majesty.

OENEUS. But are you sure you're in the right hall? This is
    the convocation of heroes for the boar hunt.

ALTHEA. Young lady, the meeting of my Royal Urn Decor-
    ating Society is this afternoon in the Acropolis South.

AGATHA. That's the big building with all the pillars just

across the courtyard.

ATALANTA. Oh, I know that, your Majesty. I'm in the right place. I've come to take part in the boar hunt. You see I've brought my bow.

OENEUS. But come on now. That's impossible. I mean, you're a girl, a maiden. Maidens don't compete with heroes on boar hunts. It's . . . it's . . . unmaidenly.

ATALANTA. I didn't read anything in the rules about the competition being limited to men.

OENEUS. Let me see those rules. Does anyone have a copy of those confounded rules?

HERALD. Right here, your Majesty. (He hands OENEUS a scroll from the table.)

OENEUS (reading scroll). . . . "Will give half the kingdom to anyone who removes said boar . . . contest open to anyone . . ."

ATALANTA. You see, your Majesty. Sex isn't even mentioned.

OENEUS. Of course sex isn't mentioned. Sex isn't a nice word. But I never thought a girl would be interested in boar hunting. This is dangerous business, you know.

ATALANTA. I know that. I'm willing to take my chances. I know how to fight, and I'm not afraid to. I've already killed two satyrs. It's time women had a chance to prove that we can compete with men on an equal footing. You men have to learn that we are more than just homemakers and sex objects. I'm entering this contest for the honor of womenhood.

OENEUS. Why didn't I write those rules more carefully?

ALTHEA. But listen, my dear. The grand prize is the hand of the Princess Serendipity and half the kingdom. Surely you don't want that?

ATALANTA. Only the last part — half the kingdom. I want to establish a kingdom — a queendom — of women where we can be free to run our own lives without interference from men.

OENEUS. Well, I just don't know . . .

THESEUS (stepping forward). Your Majesty, may I speak?

OENEUS. Of course, Theseus. Maybe you can say something sensible.

THESEUS. Your Majesty, I represent the Heroes Union, Helenic Local 280. Hercules and Jason are members, too. Up to this time we have kept quiet, but now I feel we must register a complaint. Your Majesty, we have come here in good faith expecting this to be a regulation contest run according to the guidelines set down by our union. Well, it's been anything but that. First we get scabs like this fellow over here — (He points to DEME-TRIUS.) — taking part. Then we find out that the son of the sponsor is going to be a contestant. And now you're going to let a girl compete. I've never heard of a contest in which girls competed with men. I don't even think there's anything in our by-laws about it, but I'm sure it's a direct violation of the spirit of the H.F.H. — the Helenic Federation of Heroes. What do you say, fellows?

HERCULES. It's un-Greek.

JASON. I think it's obscene.

DEMETRIUS. I think it's unfair, too, your Majesty.

OENEUS. Well, there you have it, maiden. I'm sorry, but you can't buck the union.

ATALANTA. But you can't go back on your word. Your rules say the contest is open to anyone. These heroes knew that when they came here.

HERCULES. "Anyone" doesn't include women, as far as the union is concerned.

ATALANTA. I kind of thought this might happen. Well, I've got a union, too. (She shouts off R.) Come on in, girls. I need you!

(CASSANDRA, DEINERA and CLIO [and the other followers of ATALANTA] enter R. They are young women dressed in conventional long white dresses. They carry signs reading, "Equal Rights," "Women Are People, Too," "Give Us A Chance," etc. They form a line parading around the stage chanting, "Rights, rights, give us our rights! Rights, rights, give us our rights!")

OENEUS (rising from throne). Now wait a minute! Stop this! This is outrageous! Guards! Help! (The women ignore him. They make three turns of the stage and then form a line opposite the heroes near the stage R exit. They lean on their signs chanting, "Rights, rights, rights!" ATALANTA silences them with a wave of her hand.)

ATALANTA. There's my union, your Majesty. And there's a hundred more outside. If you keep me out of this contest, we'll picket your palace till the day you die. We'll hold rallies in your royal courtyard. And we'll boycott the Royal Urn Making Society. We'll be twice as bad as the boar. Won't we, girls?

GIRLS. Right! Hurrah! (Etc.)

CLIO. Tell it like it is, Atalanta!

DEINERA. Down with the male chauvinist boars!

CASSANDRA. Up against the wall!

OENEUS. Now wait a minute. Let's not be vindictive about this.

AGATHA. I knew it was too much to expect sense from you, Odius. You've got yourself in a fine mess this time.

OENEUS. But maidens, listen to reason. If the heroes union gets down on me, I'm in real trouble.

ATALANTA. You'll get worse from us.

GIRLS (pounding signs on the floor). Rights, rights, rights, rights!

OENEUS. I don't know what to do. I've always gotten along with the union, but I can't have this.

MELEAGER. Father, may I make a suggestion?

OENEUS. I wish somebody would.

MELEAGER. Perhaps if the heroes could see the prize for which they are competing, it might make them decide to stay in the contest in spite of the irregularities.

JASON. Yeah, that's a good idea. Where is this princess we're going to fight for? All I've seen is a line drawing. She didn't look too bad, but if she turns out to be worse than her picture, I just might withdraw no matter what. After all, I've got an Argo to outfit for a voyage.

THESEUS and HERCULES. Yeah, let's see her. (Etc.)

OENEUS. Well, all right. Herald, summon the Princess Serendipity. She's been waiting in the private antechamber. I thought you boys would want to see her sooner or later.

(The HERALD crosses L, exits and returns with SEREN- DIPITY. She is a pretty girl with long blond hair and fine features. She wears a floor-length white gown and a chaplet of flowers in her hair. She walks demurely with downcast eyes.)

HERALD. The Princess Serendipity.

OENEUS. Dippy, come up here and stand by us. I've got a surprise for you.

SERENDIPITY. Yes, father. (She crosses and mounts dias.)

OENEUS. One of these fine heroes is going to be your hus- band. Isn't that great?

SERENDIPITY. Whatever you say, father. Which one?

OENEUS. Well, we're having a contest, and the one that kills that nasty old boar that's been giving us so much trouble will get your hand in marriage.

ALTHEA. Won't that be exciting, Dippy? We can work out all the details together.

SERENDIPITY (unenthusiastically). Yes, mother.

OENEUS. Uh, yes, exciting. Well, there she is, fellows.

Isn't that worth killing a boar for?

HERCULES. Not bad, not bad.

JASON. Could we have the princess turn around?

OENEUS. Turn around, Dippy. (She obeys.) Back's just as good as the front, right, boys?

ATALANTA. Sire, I protest. You're treating the princess like a bolt of dry goods. And she's your own daughter!

AGATHA. The girl's right, Odius. This is disgraceful.

GIRLS. Boo! Shame! (Etc.)

OENEUS. Oh, nonsense! These fine fellows have come a considerable distance to help us out. They deserve a look at the reward. Besides, Dippy doesn't mind. Do you, Dippy?

SERENDIPITY. No, father, not if it will help the kingdom.

ATALANTA. Well, you should mind. Stand up for your dignity, girl.

GIRLS. Hurrah! Right on! (Etc.)

OENEUS. Quiet, all of you! I've a good mind to send you all to the royal kitchen and make you clean the dishes after we've eaten the boar one of these heroes will kill.

ATALANTA. You just try it.

OENEUS. Don't tempt me. Now, gentlemen, are you in the contest or not?

THESEUS. Is she going to be in it?

ATALANTA. You can't keep me out.

OENEUS. By Zeus, I can if I want to. It's my contest. I can make the rules any way I want.

GIRLS (pounding signs). Rights! Rights! Rights!

OENEUS. Now cut that out!

MELEAGER. Father, may I speak again?

OENEUS. Why not? We seem to be rather short on decorum this morning.

MELEAGER. Well, I don't see what you're all making such a fuss for. I mean, if the boar is as bad as you claim, and these heroes are as good as they claim, a girl doesn't stand a chance of winning the prize anyway . . .

ATALANTA. I have as good a chance as anybody.

MELEAGER. . . . so why not let her compete? All she'll do is make a fool of herself.

ATALANTA. I will not.

OENEUS. By Mars, that sounds sensible.

ATALANTA. It is not sensible.

OENEUS. What do you say, fellows? After all, this silly girl could cause me a lot of trouble.

THESEUS. Well, I don't know. What do you think, men? (THESEUS, JASON and HERCULES go into a huddle. DEMETRIUS tries to join it but is forcibly excluded.) Your Majesty, considering what Prince Meleager has just said, and considering the — uh — prize at hand, we have decided that we will remain in the contest. We must state, however, that this is a special concession to your Highness and that our action is in no way meant to establish a precedent. Right, men?

JASON and HERCULES. Right.

OENEUS. Well, thank heavens that's settled. Now, why don't you all just run along and sign the entry papers? Then I'll have the military boys brief you on the boar. Go on now before somebody thinks of some other fool objections. Show them out, Herald. (Exit HERALD, JASON, THESEUS, HERCULES, DEMETRIUS, MELEAGER, ATALANTA and her followers R.) Ye gods, what a bunch of quibblers. You'd think they were buying a used chariot rather than entering an heroic contest.

ALTHEA. It's your own fault, Ony. You should have made the rules explicit. "Open only to union heroes." That would have prevented all the trouble.

OENEUS. Well, I'm not experienced at this sort of thing. How did I know that every character who can lift a spear would want a crack at the pig? Where did that fool girl come from anyway?

SERENDIPITY. I've heard of her. Her father had his heart set on a boy when she was born. He was so angry at having a girl that he abandoned her in a forest.

OENEUS. From what I've seen of her so far, that was sound thinking.

SERENDIPITY. The animals raised her, and she's got quite a reputation for competing with men in almost everything. She's made a lot of speeches, too, saying that women are just as good as men.

OENEUS. Sounds like a dangerous radical to me.

SERENDIPITY. Some of the things she says sound kind of sensible to me — I mean, a little.

OENEUS. How do you know so much about her and what she says?

SERENDIPITY. Oh, my maids talk. You know . . .

OENEUS. Well, don't listen to them. They're a bunch of featherbrains, all of them. But enough of this chit-chat. Since there doesn't seem to be any more court business, I can get back to my catapults. Come, ladies, I'll escort you to your quarters.

SERENDIPITY. Father, may I stay behind here for a little?

OENEUS. What, alone? Here in the royal hall?

SERENDIPITY. Yes, I . . . uh . . . I'm making slipcovers for your thrones, and I want to take some measurements.

ALTHEA. But, my dear, we just had the thrones reupholstered last year.

SERENDIPITY. I know, mother, but we want to keep them nice, don't we? Besides, I have so little to do.

OENEUS. Don't bother the girl, Althea. If she wants to make slipcovers for the boar, I don't care. It'll keep her from listening to her maids.

AGATHA. Bad news. He's being sensible again.

ALTHEA. Now, mother . . . Don't be too long, Dippy.

SERENDIPITY. I won't. (OENEUS rises and takes Althea's hand.)

OENEUS. Come along, dear. You know Dippy will be all right. She's a good girl.

(OENEUS, ALTHEA and AGATHA exit L. As soon as they are gone, SERENDIPITY runs to the door at R. She peers out in all directions, then seeing nothing, she returns and paces the floor nervously at C. DEMETRIUS enters R, pauses, and looks about uncertainly.)

DEMETRIUS. Dippy?

SERENDIPITY (starting). Oh! Demetrius.

DEMETRIUS. Are they all gone?

SERENDIPITY. Yes, come in quick.

DEMETRIUS (crossing and embracing her). Darling, it's so hard to get to see you alone.

SERENDIPITY (pulling free). Please, Demetrius. Somebody might come.

DEMETRIUS. I don't care. I don't care who knows I love you.

SERENDIPTIY. Well, you should. If father found out, he'd feed you to the boar.

DEMETRIUS. Just because of his stupid prejudice. What's he got against poets, anyway? My ancestors are as noble as his.

SERENDIPITY. Darling, you know father wants me to marry a hero. Besides, this boar thing has come up now. He's promised me as the prize, and he couldn't go back on his word even if he wanted to.

DEMETRIUS. That Atalanta girl is right. This whole thing is outrageous. You're put up like a used horse. I'm surprised they didn't ask your measurements.

SERENDIPITY. They were on the notices daddy sent out.

DEMETRIUS. It's disgusting. I don't see why you stand for it.

SERENDIPITY. But what can I do?

DEMETRIUS. You know very well what you can do. You can run away with me. Your father doesn't watch you at all. We could be in Persia before he'd even know you were gone.

SERENDIPITY. Demetrius, we've been all over that before. My father doesn't watch me because he trusts me. And I intend to be worthy of that trust.

DEMETRIUS. But he's so unworthy of you. He's treating you like a stuffed bear at a side show. (He throws himself on Oeneus' throne, one leg over an arm.)

SERENDIPITY (very seriously). Demetrius, get out of that throne.

DEMETRIUS. Why? Your old man is working on his catapults. He won't catch me.

SERENDIPITY. I don't care. If you love me, get up.

DEMETRIUS (rising). Oh, all right.

SERENDIPITY. Now listen, Demetrius. We've been all over this before, but I'll tell you one more time. I know you don't like my daddy, but whether you like him or not, he is the king and he is my father, and I'm bound to love and respect him on both counts. And so are you, really.

DEMETRIUS. I know, but how can I respect him when he pulls stunts like this? He's inefficient, incompetent and insensitive. And he hates my poetry.

SERENDIPITY. But he's trying, Demmy, really he is. He's doing the very best he can. I don't think he really wants to auction me off to the highest bidder, but this is the only way he knows to get rid of that awful boar.

DEMETRIUS. Well, it's a poor way to handle it, if you ask me.

SERENDIPITY. Besides, I don't see what you're so excited about. This is our big chance. All you have to do is kill the boar and daddy will have to let us get married.

DEMETRIUS. Oh, yeah, big chance. You know I'm no fighter. Listen, in the javelin qualifying trials this year I came in fifty-second out of fifty-three men.

SERENDIPITY. Well, at least you were better than someone.

DEMETRIUS. No, the fifty-third man couldn't compete. He had a wounded shoulder, and it was wounded because in the archery qualifications I missed the target altogether and hit him.

SERENDIPITY. Well, you've got to try anyway, Demetrius. Maybe Meleager or the girl will kill the boar, and at least I won't have to marry one of those awful heroes.

DEMETRIUS. That's about all we've got to hope for. (He advances to her and takes her in his arms.) Oh, come on, Dippy, run away with me. We can't take chances like that with our future.

SERENDIPITY (responding to him). You know I'd love to, Demmy. I really would. (They kiss.)

(ATALANTA enters R, fuming.)

ATALANTA. Men! Dirty, rotten, cheating men! Oh, pardon me. (SERENDIPITY and DEMETRIUS spring apart.)

DEMETRIUS. Pluto! What are you doing here?

ATALANTA. I'd ask you two the same question, but the answer is fairly obvious. I'm looking for King Oeneus. My heroic competitors won't give me a chance to see any of the information on the boar.

SERENDIPITY. I told you somebody would come, Demetrius.

DEMETRIUS. Listen, maiden, I know what you think you saw, but you're wrong. The princess here — uh — slipped, and I was just helping her to her feet.

ATALANTA. Oh, sure. You wouldn't believe the number of men who have offered to help me like that. Thank the gods I've been able to get to my own feet. So the little princess is more than a paper doll after all. Hanky-panky right in the Royal Throne Room. I owe you an apology, sister. You've got more guts than I gave you credit for.

SERENDIPITY. I'm not your sister, but thank you.

DEMETRIUS. If you approve of what we were doing, I'm sure you'll help us keep it a secret.

ATALANTA. Well, I can't say I exactly approve. Usually I'm against hanky-panky on principle. The woman always comes out the loser. But if that's what a woman wants, she should have the right to choose her own man.

DEMETRIUS. Look, if you promise to keep quiet about what you've seen, we'll help you get the boar. That's what you want, isn't it?

ATALANTA. Why should you help me? You're one of my rivals.

DEMETRIUS. Right, but I was just telling the princess here, I haven't got a chance of getting the thing myself. If you kill it, at least her father won't make her marry one of those heroes.

SERENDIPITY. I can get you all the inside information on what we know of the boar's habits.

DEMETRIUS. And if I come across it while we're in the forest, I'll try to drive it your way.

ATALANTA. Well, you two seem like nice kids and I'll keep quiet, but I don't want any special help. You could help me get the information the others are getting, though.

DEMETRIUS. We'll get you that and more. Is it a deal?

ATALANTA. It's a deal. (The three shake hands.)

SERENDIPITY. Come on, Demmy. If we hurry we can get to the briefing before it breaks up.

(SERENDIPITY and DEMETRIUS exit R. ATALANTA watches them go. Then she strolls about the room, hands behind her back. She eyes the thrones for a bit. Finally she goes up and sits in Oeneus' throne. She takes the

bow from her back, selects an arrow, notches it and sights
along it in the general direction of the R exit. MELEAGER
enters R.)

MELEAGER. Don't shoot. (Startled, ATALANTA lets the
arrow go. MELEAGER ducks.)
ATALANTA. Oh!
MELEAGER. Hey, be careful with that thing. Don't you
know it's illegal to shoot off bows in the Royal Throne
Room?
ATALANTA. Don't you know it's stupid to startle people
when they have weapons in their hands?
MELEAGER. A foot to the right and that thing would have
ruined my day. What were you shooting at me for, anyway?
ATALANTA. I wasn't shooting at you. If I had been, I'd
have hit you. Now go about your business.
MELEAGER. You are my business. I've been looking all
over for you.
ATALANTA. Looking for me? What do you want with me?
MELEAGER (producing a scroll). I thought you might want
this dope on the boar. I managed to get copies from the
briefing. If you come down from there, I'll give this to
you.
ATALANTA (not moving). Why should you want to give me
information?
MELEAGER. Well, it seems to me if father is going to hold
this silly contest, it should be run fairly. I saw what the
others did to you back there.
ATALANTA. Why didn't you say something then? Why
sneak around when it's all over?
MELEAGER. Look, I may be able to handle the boar, but I
sure can't handle Hercules, Theseus and Jason all at once.
Now do you want this stuff or don't you?
ATALANTA. I don't know. What do I have to do to get it?

MELEAGER. Absolutely nothing.

ATALANTA. People don't give help to their competition for nothing. What do you want from me?

MELEAGER. I don't want anything from you, you silly girl. I just thought I'd see the game played fairly, that's all.

ATALANTA. Oh, I get it. "Silly girl." It's like you said before. You don't think I have a chance to get that boar. That's why you're helping me. Give her all the help she wants, and then laugh when she falls flat on her face.

MELEAGER. Look, I just said those things then to get them to let you in the contest.

ATALANTA. But you don't think I'll get the boar, do you? Do you?

MELEAGER. Well, no. But that doesn't mean I'll laugh at you. As a matter of fact, I don't think I've got much chance of getting it either.

ATALANTA. You're just like all the other men. You think because I'm a woman, I'm foolish and weak and incompetent in important things.

MELEAGER. Look, I don't know you at all. I try not to judge people by appearances. But I do think you're foolish if you refuse help when it's handed to you for nothing.

ATALANTA. Nothing? That's a laugh. If you don't want to laugh at me, then you want something else.

MELEAGER. What?

ATALANTA. You know.

MELEAGER. Oh, come on. You're not my type.

ATALANTA. Well, just what is your type?

MELEAGER. I don't know, but it's not you. I like my women a little more feminine.

ATALANTA. You mean weak, foolish and helpless. A little silly — giddy — but obedient. Well, I'm not that type of woman. I'm just as good as any man. I can shoot as straight, throw the javelin as straight, and I can think straighter. And when we meet the boar, I'll prove it.

MELEAGER. Wonderful, but ths information I've got here will help anybody. Listen, all I did was come here and try to give you a fair deal, and all you've done is suspect my motives and lecture me on women's rights. Now if you want this stuff, get out of my father's throne and come down here and get it.

ATALANTA. No. No, if you really want to give me a "fair deal," you come up here and lay those papers at my feet. See how you feel kneeling to a woman for a change.

MELEAGER. Lady, you don't want a fair deal. You want revenge, and you won't get that from me. (He drops the scrolls and exits R.)

ATALANTA (standing, furious). Yes! Yes, I want revenge. I want revenge for the centuries men have dominated women. I want revenge for being considered second-rate just because I wasn't born a man. I want revenge for being left in the forest because girls aren't important and don't count. And by all the goddesses, I'll get revenge, too!

(CLIO, CASSANDRA and DEINERA enter R.)

CLIO. Atalanta! Atalanta! We've been looking all over for you.

CASSANDRA. Get yourself ready. The boar's on a rampage in a peasant village only a mile and a half from here.

DEINERA. Theseus and Jason are out already, and the others are starting.

ATALANTA. A chance. That's all I want! Come on, girls. Here's where we show them what women can really do. There'll be pork chops for supper tonight! (They all rush off L cheering. Lights dim.)

SCENE TWO

SCENE: A forest clearing. The stage is bare except for a
backdrop of trees and a large rock RC. Clumps of bushes
mask entrances R and L. It is several hours later. The boar
roars offstage L. [This is a series of highly-amplified
pig grunts.]

AS LIGHTS COME UP: THESEUS and HERCULES enter R.
They carry spears and are out of breath.

HERCULES. Hurry up, Theseus. He must be right up ahead.
THESEUS. Wait up. I'm out of breath. (He sits on the
rock.)
HERCULES. Me, too. Have you ever seen anything like that
pig?
THESEUS. That boar's something else.
HERCULES. What a monster! I had a clear shot at him
once, but he caught my spear in his teeth and broke it clean
in two. That was a large caliber spear, too.
THESEUS. I'm beginning to wonder if it's worth it. I mean,
the girl's good-looking and all, but I'm kind of fond of my
arms and legs.
HERCULES. Well, you can back out if you want to. Me,
I'd just as soon not have that Atalanta dame laughing at
me and calling me chicken.
THESEUS. Yeah, I guess you're right. Well, at least she
hasn't any chance of getting the prize.

(JASON enters R, limping and holding a bloody bandage to hs leg.)

JASON. Blast! Blast! Blast! (THESEUS and HERCULES rush to help JASON.)

THESEUS. Did he get you, man?

JASON. What does it look like? Skewered me like a shish-kabob. Thought I had him, but he was too quick for me.

HERCULES. Sit down here and let's have a look at that leg. (HERCULES and THESEUS help JASON to the rock and examine his leg.)

JASON. How does it look?

THESEUS. You're going to die, but there'll be pain first.

JASON. Oh, that's all I need, a comedian.

HERCULES. It's just a scratch. But a couple of more inches and . . .

JASON. I don't know about you fellows, but I've had it. That thing's not human.

THESEUS. But what about Atalanta?

JASON. What about her? If we can't kill that thing, it's a cinch she's not about to. We'll just tell Oeneus the whole business is impossible. Look, it's in the union regulations. All we're expected to do is make an honest effort.

HERCULES. What about the other two?

THESEUS. The poet and the college boy? They've got less chance than the girl if you ask me.

HERCULES. Yeah, I guess you're right. Well, I'm not keen on having boar tusk as a permanent part of my anatomy. If you guys are going to throw in the towel, I'll go along.

JASON. Now you're talking sense.

THESEUS. Come on, let's go. That thing could charge us any minute.

JASON. I don't think I can walk any further on my leg. (The boar roars loudly off L. THESEUS and HERCULES runn off R. JASON leaps up and limps quickly after them.)

Wait for me! Wait for me! (He exits.)

(After a count of five, during which the boar roars several
    times, ATALANTA, CLIO, CASSANDRA and DEINERA
    enter R. ATALANTA is carrying her bow.)

CLIO. If they hadn't started before you got there, you'd
    have a chance, Atalanta.
DEINERA. That's men for you. Never play fair.
ATALANTA. You have to expect that, girls. But we'll beat
    them anyway.
CASSANDRA. Atalanta, look at this. (She points to ground
    near the rock.)
ATALANTA (kneeling and examining). Blood! Oh, Minerva,
    someone's gotten it and I never even got a look at it. (The
    boar roars offstage.) No, they haven't. Not yet anyway.
    Go on back to town now, girls. You know the rules. I
    have to kill this thing by myself.
CLIO. But, Atalanta, we want to stay with you.
DEINERA. We're all sisters together.
CASSANDRA. We've sworn an oath.
ATALANTA. But you know if you're with me when I kill
    it, they'll all say I cheated. (The boar roars very loudly
    offstage.)
CASSANDRA. On the other hand . . .
CLIO. Maybe you're right.
DEINERA. We wouldn't want to hurt your chances. (The
    boar roars loudly again. DEINERA, CASSANDRA and
    CLIO scream and run off L. ATALANTA is left alone.
    There is a rustling in the bushes offstage L.)
ATALANTA. It's coming. It's really coming. (She takes an
    arrow from her quiver and notches it.) Artemis, guide my
    arrow! (The rustling grows louder. ATALANTA takes
    careful aim and shoots offstage L. The boar roars loudly.)
    Did I hit it? I can't see where my arrow went.

(MELEAGER enters L, holding the arrow in his hand.)

MELEAGER. You know, I'm getting a little tired of being shot at.

ATALANTA. Oh, heavens! I thought you were the boar.

MELEAGER. Yes, we look so much alike.

ATALANTA. What are you doing following me, anyway?

MELEAGER. I wasn't following you. I was trying to follow the boar. By the sound of him, he's right around here somewhere.

ATALANTA. I wonder where the others are.

MELEAGER. I passed Theseus, Hercules and Jason about two hundred yards back that way running in the opposite direction. They looked like they were scared to death.

ATALANTA. Some heroes. But where's Demetrius? He was supposed to drive the boar to me.

MELEAGER. I imagine he's run off, too, by now.

(DEMETRIUS runs on L. He runs directly across and off R. Then he comes back on R.)

DEMETRIUS. Atalanta, is that you?

ATALANTA. Demetrius?

DEMETRIUS. Atalanta, you know I told you I'd drive the boar to you?

ATALANTA. Yes?

DEMETRIUS. Well, I'm not exactly driving it, but it's coming. It's chasing me. Help! Stop it! (He cowers behind the rock. The boar roars offstage L.)

MELEAGER. It is coming. I caught a glimpse of it just then.

ATALANTA (drawing another arrow). It's my big chance.

MELEAGER. Now look, Atalanta, this is going to be dangerous. You'd better let . . .

ATALANTA (covering MELEAGER with the bow). Now you look. That boar is mine. Demetrius promised him to me.

I mean it, Meleager. I'll put an arrow in the man who gets between that pig and me. Stay here, both of you. I'll bring him back.

(ATALANTA moves off L, walking cautiously with bow at the ready. There are a series of roars from the boar, followed by one very loud roar and a scream from ATALANTA. She then runs back on L.)

ATALANTA. Meleager! Meleager!

MELEAGER. What's the matter? Did you miss?

ATALANTA. No, not exactly. I hit him, but I didn't kill him. I just hurt him and made him madder. Oh, he's terrible and he's coming after me. Stop him, Meleager! (She joins DEMETRIUS behind the rock.)

MELEAGER. Well, at least you got his attention. I'll see what I can do.

(MELEAGER exits L. There is another series of roars, then one great one, followed by a series of gurgling and snuffling sounds. MELEAGER enters L, shaken, half in shock.)

MELEAGER. I got him. I really got him.

ATALANTA (not moving from behind the rock). Are you sure?

MELEAGER. Yes. It wasn't even too hard. Your arrow slowed him down. All I had to do was . . . (He gestures with his spear hand.)

DEMETRIUS (rising). Let me see. (He cautiously crosses L and peers offstage.) Uh, you got him all right. What a sight!

ATALANTA. I don't want to see it.

MELEAGER. I thought you were the mighty hunter.

ATALANTA. I was — until that thing turned on me.

MELEAGER. Well, you did your part. Your arrow hit him

squarely.

DEMETRIUS. And I helped. I got him here.

MELEAGER. Yes, I think there's going to be enough boar for all three of us.

DEMETRIUS. Shall we go and drag him back with us?

MELEAGER. No, leave him. We'll send some peasants out to get him. After all, we're hunters — not butchers.

DEMETRIUS. You know, I can hardly wait to see how those great heroes — Theseus, Hercules and Jason — are going to take this. Imagine being shown up by a student, a girl and a poet.

ATALANTA. We're just as good as they are. We showed them that.

MELEAGER. Better. But let's get back and spread the happy word. I have a feeling old Calydon is going to rock tonight.

DEMETRIUS (striking a pose). Forward the heroes! Way for the mighty men of old!

ATALANTA. And the women! Don't forget the women! (They march off R, arm-in-arm with exaggerated steps.)

CURTAIN

ACT TWO

SCENE ONE

SCENE: The Royal Throne Room. Two hours later.

AT RISE OF CURTAIN: The room is empty. THESEUS, JASON and HERCULES enter R. THESEUS sits on the dias before the thrones. JASON and HERCULES move about the room, sometimes joining THESEUS. Throughout their conversation all three strike muscular poses, do sit-ups and push-ups and isometric exercises and generally act like characters from "Muscle Beach."

JASON. I can't believe it. I just can't believe it.

HERCULES. Who would? Imagine — a college boy, a poet and a girl! A rotten girl! It's just not right. There's not even anything in the union by-laws to cover this.

THESEUS. Well, you'd better believe it, both of you. The rest of the kingdom does, and the boar's carcass is lying out there to prove it.

JASON. How in the world am I going to be able to go back home? I'm going to have to turn in my card, fellows. I'll never live this down.

HERCULES. You won't? How about me? I'm supposed to be the son of Zeus, Father of Gods and Men. What do you think my daddy is going to say when he finds out his son has been shown up by a girl? He's pretty free with those thunderbolts of his as it is.

THESEUS. Well, sitting around here bellyaching isn't going to help any.

JASON. I suppose you know something better?

THESEUS. As a matter of fact, I have been thinking of a few things we could do.

HERCULES. What things? I've been thinking of some myself, but I don't think I'm really cut out to be a hermit or a shepherd in the desert.

THESEUS. You may not have to. Look, what's basically our problem? Somebody else got the boar and we didn't, right?

JASON. Not just somebody. Three particular somebodies.

THESEUS. But somebodies nevertheless. Look, would it have bothered you if I had got the boar?

HERCULES. Of course not. But you're a hero. It's no disgrace for one hero to lose to another.

THESEUS. Exactly. And that's just what's going to save us.

JASON. I don't get you.

THESEUS. All right — we've been shown up by a college boy, a poet and a girl. But the world doesn't have to know that's what they are. All we have to do is make them heroes — and presto! — no disgrace. After all, they've performed an heroic deed. Who has to know whether they were heroes before or after they did what they did?

HERCULES. Hey, you might have something there!

JASON. I don't know. You think the union would buy that?

THESEUS. Why not? There's a recruiting drive on, you know.

JASON. Yeah, and I can see them letting in a poet and a college boy, but a girl?

HERCULES. They'd never accept a woman.

JASON. You're probably right there, but I think I've got that little problem figured out, too. One of us will have to make a sacrifice, though.

HERCULES (suspiciously). What kind of sacrifice?

THESEUS. Not really much of anything. All one of us has to do is marry Atalanta.

JASON. Marry Atalanta!

HERCULES. Are you crazy?

JASON. Why would one of us want to marry that crazy dame?

THESEUS. Well, I can think of one good reason. According to our law a husband has full control over his wife. She is his property to do with as he pleases. She has to say anything he wants her to.

JASON. Hmmm, you mean we should marry Atalanta, and then force her to keep quiet about the boar.

THESEUS. Not keep quiet exactly, just tell the story from our point of view, if you know what I mean.

HERCULES. Oh, come on now. Let's just say that one of us is willing to make this "sacrifice" as you call it. What makes you think Atalanta is going to marry anybody? From what I've seen, she doesn't think any man is worth dragging home.

THESEUS. She might change her mind if she had to marry someone to get her prize. Look, it's pretty obvious King Oeneus isn't thrilled that half his kingdom is going to be ruled by a girl. All we have to do is get him to dream up some law that any ruler in Calydon has to be married, and if Atalanta wants to rule, she'll have to go along.

HERCULES. I don't know. It's a long shot. Suppose she does go along with this law. She'd probably wouldn't pick one of us.

THESEUS. Not if we get the law to read ". . . has to be a union hero or married to one." We're the only union heroes around. It'll have to be one of us.

JASON. I suppose it could work. But how're we going to decide who takes the plunge?

HERCULES. I'd rather go after another boar, myself.

THESEUS. Well, look at it this way. It may be bad at first,

but in a couple of years this whole thing will be forgotten.
There's no law that says a man can't ditch his wife when
he feels like it. I've done it myself a couple of times.

HERCULES. That's true. But still, I'd rather not be Mr.
Atalanta. You still haven't said how we're going to decide
who gets stuck.

THESEUS. Well, why don't we leave it up to Atalanta?
After all, a woman should have some say in who she's
going to marry.

JASON. Hmm, you never can tell about women . . . But
that would make the odds two to one.

THESEUS. Are you guys game?

HERCULES. What else can we do? But I still don't think
it's fair. I'm obviously the best catch around.

JASON. That's a laugh. She'll pick me if she has any sense.
But look, no cheating. Each of us has to act as much like
husband material as possible.

THESEUS. Right. Okay, gentlemen, let's shake on it. (The
three shake hands.)

(OENEUS, ALTHEA and AGATHA enter R.)

OENEUS (in a rage). So there you are, you frauds, you
hypocrites, you fakers!

ALTHEA. Now, Ony, don't lose your temper. (OENEUS
walks quickly to is throne and takes a seat. ALTHEA and
AGATHA follow him.)

OENEUS. Lose my temper! Lose my temper! I try to run
a legitimate contest, and what do I get? A bunch of reed-
paper heroes who sell out to the highest bidder.

THESEUS. Your Majesty, are you implying that we did not
make an honest effort to win the contest?

OENEUS. I'm not implying anything. I'm telling you straight
out. You threw it. You took a dive. Well, you're not
going to get away with it. I'm arresting all three of you for

corrupt practices. My guards are waiting outside.

THESEUS. Now just a minute, your Majesty. Let's not be hasty. Remember the union.

OENEUS. The union! You'll be lucky if you're still in the union when they hear about this. Besides, you're all going to spend a good long time in the dungeons — the lower dungeons, the ones with black rats and spiders in them.

HERCULES. I don't see what's bugging you so much. You got your boar killed.

OENEUS. Oh, sure, I got my boar killed. And what else have I got? I've got my daughter engaged to a namby-pamby poet, I've got a girl claiming half my kingdom, and I've got my blockhead of a son saying he did the whole thing just for the honor of it. That's what I've got. But I've also got you three, and that's some satisfaction any-way.

THESEUS. But, your Majesty, if you will just give us a chance, we think we have the solution to those little . . . uh . . . problems.

OENEUS. Solution, huh? What are you going to do? Bring the boar back to life?

THESEUS. No, your Majesty. Uh . . . if I might speak with you privately?

OENEUS. I've spoken with you all I want. The next sound I want to hear out of you is a scream of pain.

AGATHA. Now, Odius, you got yourself into this in the first place. You're the one who botched the rules of the contest. I don't think things have worked out nearly as badly as you seem to. But if you're unhappy, why don't you listen to the man?

ALTHEA. Mother's right, dear. It's only fair he have his say.

OENEUS. Confound it, Althea, I don't feel fair this morning. I don't even feel good. Oh, all right, come up here and say what you have to. But don't make any travel plans.

The spiders are still waiting. (THESEUS goes up to the throne and whispers in Oeneus' ear.) Right, so? . . . Yeah . . . yeah . . . you could? . . . you would? . . . that's right . . . it might . . . well, I don't know . . . yeah? . . . yeah . . . yeah! By Zeus, you may have something there.

AGATHA. What's he saying, Odius?

THESEUS. Remember, your Majesty, this is just between us.

OENEUS. Right. I'm sorry, ladies, but this is men's business. Theseus, this crazy plan of yours just might work.

THESEUS. I'll guarantee it, sire.

OENEUS. You'd better, or it'll still be the dungeon. But I'll take a chance.

ALTHEA. Ony, what did he say?

OENEUS. Oh, he said a lot of things, light of my life. A lot of things.

AGATHA. But we want to know. We demand to know!

OENEUS. Now you look here, mother. You wanted me to listen to this man, and I have. Our business is very private, and not to be meddled in by meddling females. You'll find out everything in good time.

AGATHA. But, Odius . . .

(The HERALD enters R.)

HERALD. Your Majesties, the boar slayers are finished with their press conference and await outside.

OENEUS. Oh, yes, yes. Send them in. Send them in. We have a number of little surprises for them.

ALTHEA. But, Ony . . .

OENEUS. Quiet, Althea.

(MELEAGER, DEMETRIUS and ATALANTA enter R. They approach the throne, kneel and rise.)

HERALD. The royal boar slayers, your Majesty.

OENEUS. Yes, yes. Well, hail the conquering heroes, eh?

MELEAGER. Thank you, father. We're glad we could be of service.

OENEUS. Oh, you have been, son. You certainly have been. And we're grateful, too. Aren't we, Althea?

ALTHEA. We certainly should be.

OENEUS. Now I suppose you're all ready for your little prizes?

MELEAGER. Father, I've told you and I've told everybody that I did my part simply for the honor of Calydon. My friends here, however, feel they have the right to claim the rewards you promised them.

DEMETRIUS. That's right. And for my share I claim the hand of the Princess Serendipity.

ATALANTA. And I claim one half of this entire kingdom to rule as I see fit.

OENEUS. Of course, of course. But first we have an extra bonus surprise for you. Theseus . . .

THESEUS. Uh, yes. Meleager, Demetrius, because of the bravery and martial skill you two have displayed in solving the – uh – little problem of the Calydonian boar, I, as representative of the Helenic Federation of Heroes, proudly extend to you an invitation to join our honorable association with the rank of Hero First Class.

OENEUS. Hey now, isn't that something? I'll tell the world!

DEMETRIUS. But I'm no hero – I'm a poet.

THESEUS. My boy, when you faced that rampaging animal, you were a hero. Right, fellows?

JASON and HERCULES. Right!

MELEAGER. I don't know. I don't know if I want to be a hero or not. If you guys are representative, it doesn't seem like much of an honor to me.

HERCULES. It's not just the honor, kid. There are all kinds of benefits – group hospitalization, death benefits, and you get a jazzy free lion skin like this.

MELEAGER. Hmm. But look, three of us killed the boar.
What about Atalanta here? You haven't asked her to
join.

DEMETRIUS. That's right. I'm not taking any honor unless
it goes to all three of us.

THESEUS. Oh, come now. Surely you can see our position.
This membership entitles you to free use of locker rooms
all over the Aegean Sea. The Helenic Federation of Heroes
is as ready to honor women as any, but we just simply
lack the facilities.

ATALANTA. Don't worry about me, fellows. I wouldn't
want to join an association of men anyway. But someday
your precious federation will be open to anyone, regardless
of sex.

OENEUS. I wish you wouldn't use that word, my dear. Now
really, Meleager and Demetrius, you can't refuse this high
honor that these men want to bestow on you.

MELEAGER. Well, if it means so much to everyone.

DEMETRIUS. I guess it wouldn't hurt. But I'm not going to
wear that stupid lion's skin. I refuse to wear the lion skin!

OENEUS. Fine, fine. You two run along now. Theseus here
tells me there'll be a little initiation ceremony tonight.

DEMETRIUS. Wait a minute. What about my prize?

OENEUS. Uh, yes . . . what prize was that?

DEMETRIUS. The hand of the Princess Serendipity.

OENEUS. Oh, right, right. Yes, well, marriage is not to be
entered into lightly, my boy, and remember the Princess
has some rights in this matter.

ALTHEA. That's the first time I've ever heard you mention
Dippy's rights.

OENEUS. Why, of course Dippy has rights. I'm not going to
marry off my daughter against her will. Listen, young man,
you get my daughter's consent, and I'll be glad to give
you her hand.

DEMETRIUS. Well, at least that shouldn't be too hard. I'll

go find her.

OENEUS. Excellent. Now you both run along. Tonight will
be a big night for both of you. (MELEAGER and DEME-
TRIUS exit R.)

ATALANTA. Well now, your Majesty, about my prize. I'm
ready to take possession of my half of the kingdom. I'll
have some changes made. In the first place, I want all
males out of my country immediately. I intend to set up
a land of women, by women, and for women.

OENEUS. Now now, not so fast. There is one slight technicality.

ATALANTA. I thought this was going to be too easy. What
kind of technicality?

OENEUS. Well, it's just a minor point, really. I should have
mentioned it before, but it slipped my mind.

AGATHA. Odius, what kind of mischief are you dreaming
up?

OENEUS. Mischief? Would I dream up mischief? No, it's
just that we have this little law in Calydon that says any
woman who would rule over Calydonian subjects must have
an escort worthy of her royal estate.

ATALANTA. What does that mean?

OENEUS. It means, my dear, that if you are going to be a
queen in Calydon, you're going to have to have a royal —
or at least a noble — husband.

ATALANTA. A husband? Never.

ALTHEA. Oeneus, I've never heard of any such law.

OENEUS. It's under section twenty-four, sub-section ten of
the legal code, my love. My . . . uh . . . legal advisors
pointed it out to me just this morning.

ATALANTA. But that isn't fair.

OENEUS. Now, my dear. It's just a legal technicality, and
I've good news for you. Theseus, Jason and Hercules have
all been . . . uh . . . smitten by your charms and each says
he will be happy to marry you if you will just pick the

lucky man. Right, men?

THESEUS, JASON and HERCULES (with a noticeable lack of enthusiasm). Right.

ATALANTA. I'd rather die than marry one of those jerks.

OENEUS. Well, you really have no choice.

AGATHA. Now just a minute, Odius. What makes you think those three are worthy of Atalanta?

OENEUS. Mother, they're heroes. That automatically makes them worthy.

ATALANTA. It was supposed to make them able to kill the boar, too, but it didn't.

AGATHA. Exactly. I can't see how these three "heroes" have at all proven they're worthy to marry a queen.

THESEUS. Your Majesty, are you questioning our courage? Our manhood?

AGATHA. You got it.

HERCULES. So what do you want us to do to prove that we're "worthy" of this little snip — I mean, the future queen?

AGATHA. Well, I think there should be some kind of further contest. After all, she beat you at the boar hunt. That's your game. I think the man who marries Atalanta should be able to prove that he can beat her at her game. What sort of thing do you do best, Atalanta, dear?

ATALANTA. Well, let me see. I'm pretty good at throwing the spear, but . . . no . . . I think what I do best is run. I'll bet there's not a man alive who can catch me at the mile run.

HERCULES. Haw — I could catch you any day of the week. It wouldn't even be close.

AGATHA. Well, there it is then. Let them have a contest. The man who can beat Atalanta in the mile run will win her hand in marriage, and can join her as co-ruler of one half of Calydon.

THESEUS. But suppose we all beat her?

AGATHA. Then you can let her pick the way you were going to.

ATALANTA. And if I beat them all?

AGATHA. Then you should have the right to rule your part of the kingdom alone until a hero comes along who can beat you.

OENEUS. But I'm not sure all this is in accordance with the spirit of the law, mother.

AGATHA. If there really is such a law.

OENEUS. Oh, there is, there is. Well, I don't know — what do you say, fellows?

THESEUS. I'm willing to match myself against any woman in a race. Providing, of course, all the contestants run as fast as they can. You know what I mean, guys?

JASON. Nobody has to worry about me. I can beat this crazy dame even with my bum leg.

HERCULES. We'll all beat her, and it'll be right back where it was. Besides, it'll be revenge for the boar thing to make her look silly.

ALTHEA. What do you say, Atalanta?

ATALANTA. Hmm. They all did run pretty fast in the wood, at that, but it looks like I've no choice. All right, I'll accept.

OENEUS. Well, I guess it's going to work out all right at that. Okay, I'll lay out a course through the woods. Do any of you have any objections to tomorrow at ten?

ATALANTA. The sooner we get this farce over the better.

THESEUS. We'll be ready tomorrow at ten, your Majesty.

OENEUS. You'd better be. And one of you had better win. The black rats and the spiders are still waiting. (The lights dim.)

SCENE TWO

SCENE: A clearing in the woods. It is about 9:45 a.m. the next morning.

AS LIGHTS COME UP: DEMETRIUS and SERENDIPITY enter R.

SERENDIPITY. So this is to be the starting place?

DEMETRIUS. Right. Your father thought it would be appropriate to start the race in the same spot where we killed the boar.

SERENDIPITY. I think this whole thing is just awful, Demmy. Atalanta's done enough to win her kingdom. Father's just trying to welch out.

DEMETRIUS (sitting on rock). Well, I can see his side. After all, he never thought a woman would end up getting half his kingdom.

SERENDIPITY. What's wrong with that?

DEMETRIUS. Well, nothing, I guess. It's just that I think most people prefer a man ruler. It's hard to make heroic poems about a woman.

SERENDIPITY. I think a woman can be just as heroic as a man — and rule a kingdom just as well, too.

DEMETRIUS. You sound like you've been talking to Atalanta.

SERENDIPITY. Maybe I have. But I've been thinking, too, and I started a long time before Atalanta came here. It's time we women stood up for our rights.

DEMETRIUS. Maybe so, but I don't think you've got much
of a kick coming. You've been pretty well taken care of.
SERENDIPITY.   Maybe I'm tired of being taken care of.
DEMETRIUS. Well, you'd better not be too tired, because
I plan to take care of you for a long, long time. (He rises
to embrace her.)
SERENDIPITY (breaking free).   That's just it, Demmy.
You men all think that all a woman wants is to be pro-
tected and sheltered. But we're capable of standing on our
own feet. We're people, too.
DEMETRIUS. And very nice people. In fact, women are
my favorite people, and you are my favorite woman.
SERENDIPITY. Demmy, I'm serious.
DEMETRIUS. So am I.
SERENDIPITY. You say I've been taken care of. Well, I
have. Daddy has been very good to me, but he never pays
any attention to how I feel. He never asks my opinion on
anything. I wouldn't be marrying you now if daddy hadn't
decided on it.
DEMETRIUS. Now there's where you're wrong. Your father
specifically told me I had to get your permission before I
could marry you.
SERENDIPITY. He did? When?
DEMETRIUS.   Yesterday — in front of the whole court.
SERENDIPITY. But why didn't you tell me?
DEMETRIUS. I didn't think it was important. Considering
the way we feel about each other, it seemed a little silly
to worry about getting your permission. I mean, what's
to get?
SERENDIPITY. What's to get? You're seeking my hand in
marriage and you ask what's to get?
DEMETRIUS. Now, I didn't mean it that way, and you know
it. I just meant I know you love me, so why make a big
deal out of it?
SERENDIPITY. Why, you smug . . . man, you! You think all

you have to do is kill a boar and women will just fall at
your feet.

DEMETRIUS. Now, look, let's not get into a fight. After
all we've gone through to be able to get married, let's not
blow it now.

SERENDIPITY. We're already in a fight. I'm not so sure I
want to marry you after the terrible things you've said.

DEMETRIUS. I've said? I've said? What have I said? That I
love you and I want to marry you and take care of you for
the rest of your life. Is that so terrible?

SERENDIPITY. There you go again. "Take care of me."
I don't want you to take care of me. I want you to love
me and I want us to be equal partners the way men and
women should be.

DEMETRIUS. Equal partners? You sound just like Atalanta.

SERENDIPITY. And you sound just like Theseus. Well,
you can just take your old marriage and . . . and . . . kill
a boar with it! (She runs off L.)

DEMETRIUS (calling after her). Now wait a minute. Serendipity, wait! Women! Serendipity! (He runs off L after
her.)

(There is a count of three. Then CLIO, DEINERA and
CASSANDRA enter R.)

CASSANDRA. Well, this must be the place.

CLIO. Look around carefully, girls. You know Atalanta
told us to come on ahead and make sure there are no
tricks on the race course. (The girls look around the rock
and the bushes.)

DEINERA. Everything looks all right to me.

CASSANDRA. No strings or wires in Atalanta's way.

CLIO. No grease on the ground at the start.

DEINERA (sitting on the rock). You know, I think it's just
terrible that Atalanta has to run this race. It's an insult

to womenhood.

CLIO. We should have picketed. I like to picket. Rights! Rights! Rights!

CASSANDRA. It's fun all right, but in a way I envy Atalanta.

DEINERA. What do you mean?

CASSANDRA. Well, I know they're male chauvinists and all, but have you seen the muscles on that Hercules character! I wouldn't mind having him chasing me in the woods!

CLIO. Cassandra, what a reactionary thing to say. You should value a man for his personality, not his muscles . . . besides, Theseus is the really cute one.

DEINERA. I kind of like Jason myself. He's been a sailor. I always go for sailors.

CASSANDRA. Yeah, but all those gorgeous muscles on Hercules! Just going to waste. What a shame!

CLIO. Now, girls, we've got to stop talking this way. Remember, Hercules, Theseus and Jason are men and that makes them the enemy. What would Atalanta say?

CASSANDRA. Oh, she'd probably make a speech.

DEINERA. Well, if Atalanta wins this race, she can set up her kingdom for us girls and stop making speeches.

CASSANDRA. A kingdom of women, by women, and for women.

CLIO. Doesn't that sound wonderful?

CASSANDRA and DEINERA (without enthusiasm). Wonderful.

CASSANDRA. And dull.

CLIO. And dull. Well, cheer up. One of those heroes may beat her and she'll have to let men in. In the meantime, it's our duty to support her and cheer her on all we can.

DEINERA. Oh, you know we'll support Atalanta, Clio. We've always stuck by her, haven't we, Cassandra?

CASSANDRA. Right.

CLIO. Promise?

CASSANDRA and DEINERA (shaking hands with CLIO). We promise.

(Suddenly THESEUS, HERCULES and JASON enter R.)

THESEUS. A-ha! Just as I thought! (The three girls scream and retreat to the bushes L.) I told you guys we needed to get out here early. See, Atalanta's sent these three out here to booby trap the course.

HERCULES. Good thinking, Theseus. You can never trust a woman!

CLIO. That's a lie! We weren't out here to booby trap the course. Atalanta sent us here to make sure you guys didn't do it. (The girls come out from behind the bushes.)

JASON. A likely story! Why should anyone think we'd do something dirty like that? We're men of honor.

CASSANDRA. You didn't show much honor in the woods with the boar. Atalanta said you all ran away.

THESEUS. That's a rotten lie. We just weren't lucky enough to be in the right place at the right time, that's all.

HERCULES. Right. If I'd been there, I'd have killed the boar twice as fast as your leader and those other two.

DEINERA. Oh, la de da! Listen to the big hero talk, girls.

CASSANDRA. He talks big now, but I'll bet he ran fast in the woods. He doesn't have enough muscles to kill a boar.

HERCULES. Muscles? Who doesn't have enough muscles? (He flexes his arm.) Just look at this. You'll never see another biceps like this. Just come here and feel how hard it is!

CASSANDRA (impressed). I'll . . . I'll take your word for it.

CLIO. Besides, it takes more than muscles and good looks to kill a boar. Doesn't it, Theseus?

THESEUS. You think I'm good looking?

CLIO. Now, I didn't say that. Some girls might think so, though.

THESEUS. A lot of them have, honey. But you're not so bad looking yourself.

CLIO. Flatterer.

DEINERA. Don't listen to him, Clio. You know how sailors can flatter you.

THESEUS. I'm not a sailor.

JASON. But I am. What do you mean, sailors are flatterers?

DEINERA. Oh, you know. Sailors are always telling girls dumb things . . . like how pretty they are and how sweet they are . . . and things like that.

JASON. Well, you do seem kind of sweet.

DEINERA. See, there you go. (By this time the girls are hanging on the heroes arms, feeling their muscles, making eyes at them, etc. THESEUS suddenly breaks free from CLIO.)

THESEUS. Wait a minute! Wait a minute!

CLIO. What's the matter?

THESEUS. It's a trap! That's what it is! A trap!

HERCULES. What's a trap, Thees? What's the matter?

THESEUS. These girls, that's the trap. Atalanta sent you girls out here, didn't she? You were supposed to sweet talk us until we'd want to throw the contest. Yeah, that's what's going on. We're supposed to fall for you three so we won't want to marry Atalanta.

HERCULES (pushing CASSANDRA away). Boy, how low can you get?

JASON (pushing DEINERA from him). It almost worked, too.

CLIO. That's a lie! That's terrible! We wouldn't throw ourselves at anybody just to help Atalanta win.

CASSANDRA. I wouldn't throw myself at anybody for any reason. And I certainly wasn't throwing myself at anybody right now.

DEINERA. I've never been so insulted in my life!

CLIO. Come, girls. It's obvious we've made a terrible mistake.

CASSANDRA. Pigs! Boars!

DEINERA. To think that they thought that we thought . . . Ohhh!

CASSANDRA, CLIO and DEINERA. Men! (They exit R with their noses up in the air.)

HERCULES (sitting on the rock). Boy, that was close!

JASON. That was great thinking, Thees. Imagine playing up to us to get us to throw the contest.

THESEUS. Well, you have to watch women every minute. They're deceitful and devious and they'll stop at nothing.

HERCULES. That's because they're weak and helpless. They haven't got the strength to fight fair.

JASON. Yeah, poor things. What else can they do? If you were nothing but curves and good looks, you'd fight that way, too.

HERCULES. Like Cassandra.

THESEUS. And Clio.

JASON. And Deinera. You know, guys, they did have a clever plan.

HERCULES. Too bad it didn't work.

THESEUS (after a slight pause). Hey, I've got an idea!

HERCULES and JASON. What?

THESEUS. Let's go give them another chance at it!

HERCULES and JASON (as they exit R). Now you're talking. Oh, yeah. Let's do. (Etc.) (THESEUS follows them off.)

(Count of three. ATALANTA enters R dressed for running.)

ATALANTA. No one here yet? I wonder where the girls are. The others should be here, too. Just like men — never show up till the last minute.

(MELEAGER enters L.)

MELEAGER. Don't shoot!

ATALANTA. Shoot? I don't even have my bow.

MELEAGER. That's a relief. Every time we meet, you shoot at me.

ATALANTA. You're always popping up in the wrong place, that's all. What are you doing here anyway?

MELEAGER. I've been going over your race course. Thought my father might have arranged some nasty little surprises for you.

ATALANTA. My girls are supposed to be doing the same thing, but I don't see them any place. Are there any surprises?

MELEAGER. Not that I can find. It looks like he's going to play it straight.

ATALANTA. I think I'm insulted. He feels I'm such a sure loser he hasn't even taken the trouble to rig things. Say, what's your big concern in this all of a sudden?

MELEAGER. Oh, I don't know.

ATALANTA. You don't think I can win either, do you?

MELEAGER. I didn't say that.

ATALANTA. No, but that's what you meant. Give the little lady an even break so she can't complain when she falls flat on her face, eh? (She begins practicing racing starts. MELEAGER sits on the rock and watches.)

MELEAGER. That's what you said before the boar contest. Why do you hate us men so? We aren't all like those phony heroes, you know.

ATALANTA. I hadn't noticed. You're joining their union, aren't you?

MELEAGER. That doesn't mean I'm like them.

ATALANTA. Maybe not now, but you will be. You run around with that type long enough, and you'll get like them.

MELEAGER. Maybe. But what do you care anyhow?

ATALANTA. I don't care at all. But you asked me why I hate men. I hate them because sooner or later they all turn out to be cheats and phonies. The only thing that men are better at than women is lying and hypocrisy.

MELEAGER. Don't women ever lie, too?

ATALANTA. Not like men do.

MELEAGER. Oh, I don't know. I think all people lie pretty much alike. Look, nobody's perfect, men or women. Not even you.

ATALANTA. Thanks. I never claimed to be perfect.

MELEAGER. Just superior?

ATALANTA. But we women are superior. We live longer, we can stand pain better, and we're morally superior, too.

MELEAGER. Atalanta, who killed the boar?

ATALANTA. I did — and you — and Demetrius.

MELEAGER. Right, we all did. Yesterday in this very spot the three of us worked together, and we got the job done. Back then I didn't care if you were a monkey. I couldn't have finished that thing off if you hadn't hit it with your arrow first . . . And I think you were pretty glad I was there, too.

ATALANTA. I was weak and foolish.

MELEAGER. We all have our moments of weakness — men and women — but we have our moments of strength, too.

ATALANTA. But look at the difference. We killed the boar, but you get made into a hero, and I have to take part in this silly contest just to be able to claim my prize and live as I please.

MELEAGER. I know, and that's not right.

ATALANTA. Men always come out ahead. When I was only nine I beat all the little boys in a race, but they gave the prize to the boy who came in second. It was a beautiful golden apple. And that's the way it always is. Men always get the golden apples.

MELEAGER. Not always, but more often then they should, I guess. Well, I can't do anything about this contest but wish you luck. But cheer up. Even if you lose, marriage isn't all bad, you know.

ATALANTA. Marraige? To one of them? I'd rather die than have one of them as a husband. I'll give up my kingdom first, too.

MELEAGER. What kind of husband would you settle for?

ATALANTA. He'd have to be different. He'd have to treat me as an equal. I wouldn't have him patronizing me or looking down on me.

MELEAGER. How about love?

ATALANTA. Oh, that too, I suppose. Yes, I'd have to love him. But I couldn't love a man I can beat. He'd have to be able to beat me . . . at a contest like this . . . fair and square. He'd have to take the prize from me.

MELEAGER. Then if one of those heroes beats you today, you should be happy to marry him.

ATALANTA. Oh, you've got me all mixed up. (MELEAGER crosses to ATALANTA and puts his arms around her.)

MELEAGER. I don't think love is a question of winning or losing at all.

ATALANTA. It isn't?

MELEAGER. No. When you're in love both men and women win . . . and both lose. You always give more than you get, and get more than you give. Like this. (He kisses her.)

ATALANTA. Give more than you get? (She kisses him.)

MELEAGER (kissing her again). You see? Everybody wins.

ATALANTA (breaking away). No! No, I can't do it, Meleager! I can't give up all I've worked for. I want my prizes, my golden apples. I won't give them up! Never! (She runs off L. MELEAGER shrugs and exits R.)

(Count of five. OENEUS, ALTHEA, AGATHA and the HERALD enter R.)

OENEUS. Well, here we are. Now where in the world is everybody?

(HERCULES, JASON, THESEUS, CLIO, DEINERA and
    CASSANDRA enter R, paired off.)

THESEUS. Here we are, your Majesty. We were just . . . uh
    . . . reconnoitering the ground.
CASSANDRA (giggling). And so were we.
OENEUS. Hmm. Yes . . . well, where's Atalanta? She's
    holding things up now. Just like a woman, always late.
HERCULES. I'll bet she's chickened out. She's probably
    half way back to Greece already.

(ATALANTA enters L.)

ATALANTA. Here I am, your Majesty, all ready.
OENEUS. And only five minutes late. Remarkable. Now
    then, who's the lucky man to race this lady first?
AGATHA. First? You mean she's going to have to race them
    one at a time?
OENEUS. I . . . uh . . . I suppose that wouldn't be fair, eh?
AGATHA. It certainly wouldn't be. She'd be worn out by
    the time she raced the third man.
OENEUS. Well, I didn't think it would hurt to give it a try.
    All right, line up, all four of you.
THESEUS. We'll even give the lady the inside track.
ATALANTA. I'm not asking for any favors. (ATALANTA,
    THESEUS, HERCULES and JASON line up at the rock,
    facing offstage R. They assume starting positions.)
OENEUS. Now you know the rules: Once around the track,
    no pushing or tripping. Get ready! Get set! Go! (The
    four run offstage R [or if the director desires, they may
    run offstage entirely and out through the audience].)
ALTHEA. Oh, dear, I can't see for the trees!
OENEUS. Herald, get up on the rock and let us know what's
    happening.
HERALD. Yes, your Majesty. (He leaps to the top of the

rock, and begins calling the race like a modern race announcer.) At the far turn they're still all bunched up. It's Theseus by half a length, then Jason, and Hercules. Atalanta is boxed out on the inside . . .

AGATHA. Run, Atalanta! You can do it!

OENEUS. Come on, Theseus! (There is general cheering.)

HERALD. On the backstretch, it's Theseus by a length, then Jason, then Hercules, Atalanta trailing by half a length . . . It's still Theseus, Jason, Hercules and Atalanta! (More cheering.) At the far turn, it's still too close to call. Wait a minute! Atalanta is moving to the outside. Atalanta is making her move. She's passing Hercules . . . (Cries of encouragement from the women, groans from OENEUS.) It's Theseus, Jason, Atalanta and Hercules. Now Atalanta is passing Jason. She's drawing up on Theseus. At the stretch it's Theseus, Atalanta, Jason and Hercules. It's Theseus by half a length, Theseus by a quarter. Here they come! It's Theseus and Atalanta, Theseus and Atalanta. Now it's Atalanta in the lead. Atalanta is going to win this race!

(ATALANTA runs on from R. The girls cheer wildly. She does not appear to be breathing hard.)

ATALANTA. Morning, all. Just thought I'd run by.

(THESEUS, JASON and HERCULES run on from R, puffing and blowing.)

THESEUS. I'm sorry, your Majesty. We gave it all we had.

OENEUS. Gave it all you had! Gave it all you had! You guys have cost me a bundle in side bets. I'm out five hundred gold pieces. Oh, my gods!

HERCULES. She was just too fast for us.

JASON. I'm bushed. I don't think I can ever run again.

OENEUS. Where you're going you won't have much chance to run. There's not much room to race in the deepest dungeons.

ATALANTA. In the meantime, your Majesty, how about my prize? I now claim half of the kingdom to rule by myself since there is no man here who can beat me.

OENEUS. It looks like I don't have any choice. Who would have thought it? Half of Calydon run by a woman!

(MELEAGER enters R, dressed to race.)

MELEAGER. Just a moment, father. You have one more challenger.

OENEUS. Meleager! You?

MELEAGER. That's right. I challenge the maiden Atalanta to race — same course, same conditions.

ALTHEA. But, Meleager, you're not even a hero.

MELEAGER. You forget, mother, I was initiated into the union last night.

OENEUS. But how do you think you can beat Miss Fleet-foot here if these other fellows failed?

MELEAGER. I've lettered in track, too, father. Anyway, for the honor of Calydon, I'd like to try.

ALTHEA. What do you say to this, Atalanta?

ATALANTA. It doesn't matter to me, sire. I can run all day. But I warn you, Meleager, I want my prize. You'll have to beat me fair and square.

MELEAGER. I wouldn't have it any other way. If you get your golden apples, you'll have earned them.

OENEUS. Well, all right then. But let's get on with it. I've got a catapult to make. Get up to the line. (MELEAGER and ATALANTA take their positions.) Get ready . . . Get set . . . Go! (ATALANTA and MELEAGER run off L.)

HERALD. And in the first turn it's Meleager slightly ahead . . . Now in the backstretch it's Meleager and Atalanta . . .

Now Atalanta is pulling up . . . Atalanta is going to pass
Meleager. (Cheers from the women.) Wait a minute . . .
Meleager has dropped something . . . something round and
shiny . . . golden. Atalanta has stopped to pick it up.
Meleager is pulling away. (Cheers from the men, groans
from the women.) Now Atalanta has started running . . .
she's pulling up again . . . they're neck and neck . . .
Meleager has dropped another one of those golden things.
Atalanta is stopping again . . . In the far turn it's Meleager
by three lengths . . . But Atalanta is pulling up again . . .
At the top of the stretch they're neck and neck. There goes
another one of those shiny things. Atalanta is stopping
again. Meleager is pulling away, and it's Meleager by two
lengths!

(MELEAGER runs on R.)

OENEUS. My boy, you've done it! You've saved Calydon!

(ATALANTA runs on R, carrying three golden apples.)

ATALANTA. I should have known you'd come up with some
trick.
OENEUS. Well, maiden, tricks or no, I'd say you lost the
race. I don't know if I'm exactly pleased with my future
daughter-in-law, but at least there'll be a king in Calydon.
MELEAGER. No, father, there'll be only a queen. I fought
the boar for the honor of it; I raced just to prove a point.
If the lady wants to remain single, that's the way it will be.
ALTHEA. That's very generous of you, son.
ATALANTA. Well, I don't want your generosity. Oh, no,
you won the race, and you've got to take the consequences,
Meleager. There'll be a king and a queen in Calydon.
ALTHEA. You mean, you want to marry my son?
ATALANTA. Let's just say I live up to my agreements.

Meleager and I will rule our kingdom together. We'll each give some and take some. (To MELEAGER.) It's going to be fifty-fifty.

MELEAGER. Fifty-fifty. That's the way it will be.

OENEUS. Well, if you've made up your minds. It looks like I'll have a wedding ceremony to go over.

(SERENDIPITY enters L with DEMETRIUS following.)

SERENDIPITY. Make that two weddings, father. Demetrius here has just humbly asked for my hand in marriage, and I have graciously consented to be his bride. Isn't that right, Demetrius?

DEMETRIUS. That's absolutely right, my love.

SERENDIPITY. And we're going away together to the Aegean for our honeymoon, and then we're coming back here so Demetrius can write poetry, and I can learn to rule our half of the kingdom so that after you and mother are gone there'll be somebody to take over. Right, Demetrius?

DEMETRIUS. Anything you say, my pet.

OENEUS. Ye gods! It looks like there's going to be two queens in Calydon. Oh, well, at least one of them will be my flesh and blood.

AGATHA. And I'd say that on the whole things probably will go on at least as well as before. Welcome to the family, children.

THESEUS. Well — heh, heh — I'm certainly glad that everything has worked out so well. Guess I'll be going along now. Big union meeting tonight, you know . . .

OENEUS. Hold it, you. You're not going any place. It's the black rats and spiders for you and your two buddies for a long, long time.

CLIO. Ohhh!

CASSANDRA. Oh, dear!

DEINERA. Oh, no!

OENEUS. What's this?

CLIO. Oh, your Majesty, please don't lock him up. He's . . . he's really very nice.

CASSANDRA. And Hercules is so strong.

DEINERA. And Jason's a sailor. A sailor would rot in a dungeon.

OENEUS. Well, this is something new.

ATALANTA. Your Majesty, might I make a suggestion? (She whispers in his ear.)

OENEUS. Capital idea! Theseus, you and your two heroic friends are pardoned from prison, but there is one little chore you'll have to do. Ladies and gentlemen, in honor of the coming double marriage, I order three days of celebration and a public barbeque of the boar my . . . uh . . . children have slain. And to turn the spit we have three of the greatest heroes of the Western world, Theseus, Jason and Hercules. You can do it all together or one at a time, fellows.

THESEUS. I'm not too sure but what I'd prefer the dungeon.

JASON. Imagine the disgrace.

DEINERA. Oh, don't worry, Jason, honey. We'll be glad to help, won't we, girls?

CASSANDRA and CLIO. Oh, yes. Right. You bet. (Etc.)

OENEUS. Now come along, all of you. We have some celebrating to do! (All cheer and exit R, except MELEAGER and ATALANTA.)

MELEAGER. Well, maiden, I guess it didn't work out as you wanted, but everyone else seems happy.

ATALANTA. I'll live, but you did cheat, you know.

MELEAGER. I guess it was a dirty trick, but when you talked so much about golden apples I figured if I dropped some, they might distract you.

ATALANTA. Yes, they were very distracting. And you were right. I got them all.

MELEAGER. Put them in a safe place. I know you wanted them more than me, even if you did end up with both.

ATALANTA. Oh, I just couldn't resist them. And I'll treasure them until the day I die. They'll always be the dearest things on earth to me. (ATALANTA and MEL-EAGER embrace and kiss, ATALANTA holding the apples in her hands which go around Meleager's neck. As the curtain closes on the embracing pair, ATALANTA slowly lets each apple drop to the ground, one by one.)

CURTAIN

THE END

ALTERNATIVE ENDING
FOR ACT ONE, SCENE TWO

This following ending may be used if the director wishes to bring the dead boar on stage:

MELEAGER. Yes, I think there's going to be enough boar for all of us. Well, let's go drag our trophy home.
DEMETRIUS. You mean we're going to have to carry that thing?
MELEAGER. It's not going to follow us, that's for sure. Come on. We'll tie it to my spear. (MELEAGER and DEMETRIUS exit L.)
ATALANTA (calling after them). Be careful. It may not be dead yet.
MELEAGER (offstage). Don't worry. It's nothing but ham and bacon now.

(MELEAGER and DEMETRIUS enter L, struggling under the weight of the boar, which is trussed up to Meleager's spear.)

DEMETRIUS. This thing must weigh a ton!
MELEAGER. Buck up. It's only three miles back to the palace. Think of the expression on Oeneus' face when he sees us walk in. Old Calydon is going to rock tonight. (DEMETRIUS tries to strike a pose despite the weight of the boar.)
DEMETRIUS. Forward the heroes! Way for the men of valor!
ATALANTA. And the women! Don't forget the women! (They march off R with the boar.)

END OF ACT ONE, SCENE TWO

PRODUCTION NOTES

ACTION

ATALANTA will work best if the director gets as much action into the proceedings as possible. Theseus, Jason and Hercules should be constantly striking poses, doing exercises, and in general behaving like refugees from "Muscle Beach." Atalanta's followers should parade and chant their slogans with vigor. The killing of the boar is arranged so that all the action may take place off stage, or the boar's carcass may actually be brought on, if the director can whip up a convincing carcass. The race at the end of Act Two may also be done off stage, or the director may have the racers leave the stage and run out through and around the audience. The latter will probably be more effective but hall limitations may make it impractical or unsafe.

COSTUMES

Oeneus wears a white toga trimmed in purple. This is a loose, floor-length robe draped from the left shoulder. It can easily be made from a sheet. The Herald and Demetrius also wear togas but without the purple trimming. Meleager, Jason and Theseus wear white tunics (T-shirts will do) and short skirts which come just to the knee. Hercules wears a lion's skin draped from one shoulder and also ending at the knee. This may be worn over a white T-shirt, if desired. Atalanta wears a costume similar to that of the other heroes. The other women wear loose, floor-length dresses. Those of Althea and Agatha are trimmed in purple. The predominate color of all the costumes should be white and ornament should be kept to a minimum.

PROPS

Theseus and Jason carry long spears in all but the race

scene, and Hercules carries a club. These heroes may also wear belts with short swords and scabbards during the boar hunt and they may carry large round shields. Meleager carries a spear for the hunt, and Demetrius also has a short spear for this scene. Atalanta wears a quiver of arrows and carries a bow. Her followers carry their signs for Act One, Scene One. (Try to come up with some catchy women's liberation slogans.) The boar can be made from papier mache, cardboard, hides, etc. It should look reasonably convincing and produce an effect on the audience when it is brought on. If you cannot manage this, it would probably be better to go with the offstage option. All papers and pieces of writing in the play are in the form of scrolls. Atalanta's golden apples can be made from styrofoam or from "bean bag" material. However, they should not bounce when she drops them at the end of the play.

THE ROYAL THRONE ROOM

This is a large, sparsely furnished room. A fly or drop across the rear of the stage shows a white brick wall decorated in the center with a classical style tapestry of heroes, maidens and gods. Four Doric pillars are arranged before it. There is a low dias at stage left slanted to face the audience, which holds three thrones — those of Oeneus, Althea and Agatha. Oeneus' throne, slightly larger than the others, is in the center. The dias is covered with a purple carpet. Upstage just right of center between two columns is a small table and a chair for the Herald, who doubles as Oeneus' secretary. There are scrolls on the table, and a quill pen. Two pillars stage right and two stage left mark entrances to the room. Other classical type decorations may be added to the taste of the director, but these should not be over-done.

THE FOREST CLEARING

The stage is bare except for a backdrop, of trees and a

large rock right center. Clumps of bushes mask entrances right and left.

PRONOUNCIATIONS

Oeneus	O én i us
Meleager	Mel ée ger
Theseus	Thée see us
Deinera	Dée in era
Aegean	A gée an
Aeson	Í son

DIRECTORS NOTES

DIRECTORS NOTES